Curly Tail

Velyn Cooper

ISBN-10: 148483528X
ISBN-13: 978-1484835289

VC Productions
vcproductions1@gmail.com

Welcome

Hello,

My name is Curly.
I am a lizard.

My tail curls so I am a
Curly Tail Lizard.

I live in
The Bahamas.

Curly Tails are good.
Some people even have
them as pets.

Here I am sitting on a conch shell.

Here I am in a tree.
Can you see me?

Here I am on top of a can.

Here I am on the back of a van.

Sometimes my tail is curled.

Sometimes my tail is straight.

Sometimes I get rid of my tail and

grow a new one!

At the end of the day
after having some fun,

I climb the stairs and make my way home.

Do you know what I am?

I am a _____

I am a _____

I am a _____

I am a _____

I am a _____

I am a _____

I am a _____

Answers

Butterfly

Bee

Grasshopper

Crab

Pigeon

Stingray

Ladybug

Baby Frog

Other Children's Books by Velyn Cooper

Rusty the Rat
Let's Have Fun with Music (soon to be released)

Other books by Velyn Cooper

Biblical Journeys: Passages Through Time and Into Eternity

Expressions of Love

Happy Mother's Day

High School Girls- Build A Strong Foundation & Face Your
            Future Prepared & Courageous

High School Girls- Build A Strong Foundation & Face Your
            Future Prepared & Courageous

Look to God in Faith

My Redeemer Lives – Photo Essay

Natural Arrangements – Unity in the Midst of Diversity

Poetry From the Heart

Reflections: A 90-Day Devotional

Renewing Your Mind — Transformation is a Lifelong Process

Shades of Pink – in Memory of Hartlyn Cooper Martin

The Beauty of Freeport, Grand Bahama, Bahamas

The Journey to Becoming a True Woman of Virtue

Thoughts: A Book of Quotes

Transitioning High School and Beyond —The Journey Begins

Understanding God Through Repentance, Confession and Baptism, Salvation

What Does The Bible Say About…?

If you would like to contact the author,
please send your questions or comments to:

Velyn Cooper

P. O. Box F42524

Freeport, Grand Bahama

Bahamas

Email: **biblicaljourneys@gmail.com**

Website: biblicaljourneys.net

Be sure and check out our Kids Corner

http://www.biblicaljourneys.net/jabez-world-changers.html